Self-Healing With

The Art Of HOLOGAZING MEDITATION

Embracing Wholeness In Our Holographic Universe

JASMIN AKASH M.A.

Self-Healing With The Art Of
HOLOGAZING MEDITATION

Copyright © 2014 by Jasmin Akash M.A.

ISBN: 9780990545569
Library of Congress Control Number: 2014915865

The author of this book does not dispense medical advice or prescribe the use of any technique as a form of treatment for physical, emotional, or medical problems without the advice of a physician, either directly or indirectly. The intent of the author is only to offer information of a general nature to help you in your quest for emotional and spiritual well-being. In the event you use any of the information in this book for yourself, which is your constitutional right, the author and the publisher assume no responsibility for your actions.

Akash Khi Publishing
Kihei, Hawaii USA

For more information about Hologazing, please contact:
Jasmin Akash
info@akashkhi.com · www.akashkhi.com

ACKNOWLEDGEMENTS

My first book - *Holographic Meditation: The 12 Elixirs of Life* was published in 2001. Since then I have further developed and refined these teachings and techniques. This book is revised and expanded, containing newly discovered information and insights - the culmination of 14 years of inquiry, self-discovery and commitment.

I am grateful to all my friends, family and all those who have inspired and helped me in this process. My special thanks to Dr H. Tavakoli for supporting the Akash Khi project; Zoran C. for graphic design; James Ginsburg for editing; Sara Smith for photography; and in particular my brother and my parents for their love, their belief in me, and their incredible patience over the years as I wrote, and rewrote, and rewrote.

Contents

Chapter 3
Applying Universal Values Of Oneness

Notes
Bibliography

"The voyage of discovery is not in seeking new landscapes but in having new eyes."

- Marcel Proust

Introduction

In 1998, I quite spontaneously began weaving intricate geometric shapes with my hands and fingers. My fingers would join and interlace into symmetrical patterns as if propelled by some sort of magnetic attraction. Day after day I remained totally engrossed in this activity. I wasn't really aware of the profound impact this would have on my future, but I recognized it as an auspicious sign. I felt a spiritual intelligence from within communicating through these mystical hand gestures, animating my hands and aligning my fingers into what seemed to be random patterns. The flow was constant and effortless and I felt myself joyously surrendering into the experience. What was the purpose and deeper meaning of it all?

The urge to create the hand poses was not only constant, but I also felt they had to be perfectly symmetrical. There was always a sense of incompleteness unless both hands were equally shaped. I was striving toward balance, because it naturally felt good. In order to perfect the shapes, I would patiently measure the finest proportions with my eyes, aligning every point along the midline. This became a fine art in itself.

Each day I channeled a greater and greater variety of geometric finger configurations. But as soon as I "untied" my hands, I would forget the particular patterns that came through. Since I didn't have a teacher or any external source of information, I realized I had to let go and depend on the grace of an inner guidance. It was only through reemergence and constant repetition that I was able to learn and remember. Over time I became more and more able to effortlessly recreate hundreds of intricate hand patterns.

With practice I noticed how good it felt to hold the poses for extended periods of time. I would close my eyes, relax and simply listen to my hands. My thoughts would disappear, leaving me calm and composed, and in a meditative state.

Quan Yin's picture was hanging on a white wall in my room. Quan Yin is often referred to as the female Buddha. It was my daily routine to sit on the futon facing the picture and practice my meditation. One day, while I was totally immersed in aligning a hand pattern, I experienced a sudden shift in perception. Unexpectedly, the pattern changed into a different form and suddenly my fingers became transparent. In effect, I could see the Quan Yin right through my fingers! Although I had already been practicing for several months, I never witnessed this phenomenon before. This was truly a life-changing moment for me, triggering a "satori" experience - a state of sudden, intuitive awakening.

Taken totally by surprise, my mind was jolted into a state of heightened awareness and I experienced an "aha!" moment. I knew it was a blessing to discover this visual effect with Quan Yin's image in the background. In a flash of insight I recalled the many paintings and statues of her and the Buddha with his hands in various poses (called mudras), and I thought to myself: "Perhaps he had a similar experience. What if one day while sitting in meditation he saw through his hands the same as I was now with these newly discovered mudras?"

The Buddha taught that the material world of form is intrinsically empty, that appearances are nothing more than an illusion created by our senses. Beyond and within the external world of form there is a transcendental reality that is the source from which all creation is manifest. It's our attachment to the material which creates separation and gives rise to human suffering. Seeing through this veil of illusion awakens us to our true nature, to the essential truth of Oneness. I was pretty sure this timeless process is what I was experiencing through my hand poses.

Over the years I had wrestled with this enigmatic teaching, a riddle not easily grasped with the intellect. This visual opening gave me an alternative perspective on things. It helped me to "get it" on a deeper essential level, to intuit the meaning behind the teaching. Spiritual seekers on different paths try many different approaches. For me this shift in perception had awakened my mind to a whole new level of awareness and possibility. It was becoming a teaching in itself, but a very different kind of teaching. It was non-verbal, intuitive communication piercing directly to the heart of the matter, initiating a major breakthrough in my consciousness and profoundly changing my life path. What I was seeing became the blueprint for what I would later call the *Hologazing Technique*. Of course, at that time I didn't even dream about writing a book, let alone creating a whole new method of spiritual practice. I knew only that I was somehow being guided on this path, and that more would be revealed. I just had to remain dedicated to my evolutionary process and not be attached to any particular outcome.

After this visual revelation I had such a sublime feeling in my heart. I knew something special had happened in my life! I had absolutely no explanation about the nature of these visual effects, but I was intrigued and totally determined to find out how it all worked. I welcomed the fact that this was all completely new to me and I was irresistibly drawn to both the stimulating visual experiences and the intellectual challenge. And so, without any preconceptions I embarked on a journey of inquiry and self-discovery, wondering where this path would take me next.

Thus I began to consciously investigate this amazing geometry of vision and light. It became my daily routine for many months to come. I would place my hand before my eyes and it would turn into a wave-like transparent image. I could see the whole background through it! Then it would rhythmically alternate between solid and transparent form or even vanish completely out of sight for brief moments. I felt as if my whole body was being transformed into an empty space!

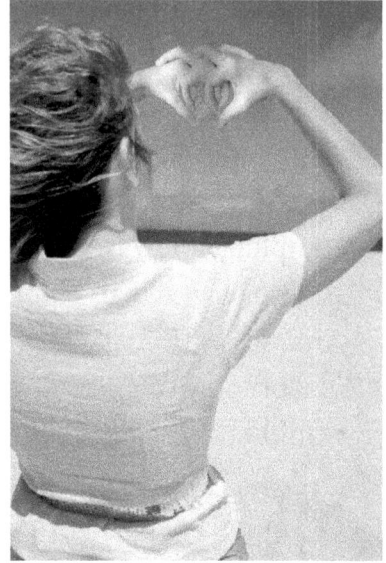

Composing my fingers into a geometric pattern I would hold it to my eyes like a kaleidoscope. With a steady, relaxed gaze I would look through it into the distance while witnessing multi-dimensional patterns emerge through my hands. By changing the poses, a variety of specific configurations were being revealed, which inspired me to contemplate their nature. They were not two-dimensional or static imagery. These visually derived patterns had a fluid, kinetic character, like pure light captured in the hands. Prolonged gazing revealed very subtle movement on which I would concentrate, paying attention to every detail.

What started out as gazing through my hands expanded to encompass various things in my surroundings. I would pick up pens, spoons, a cell phone and other objects of various textures and sizes. I found I was able to see through them as if

I had X-ray vision! I would go out in nature and experiment with leafs, flowers, and stones. I was amused to watch what happened. For example, a leaf becoming transparent, vanishing completely out of sight…then reappearing again in rhythmic intervals.

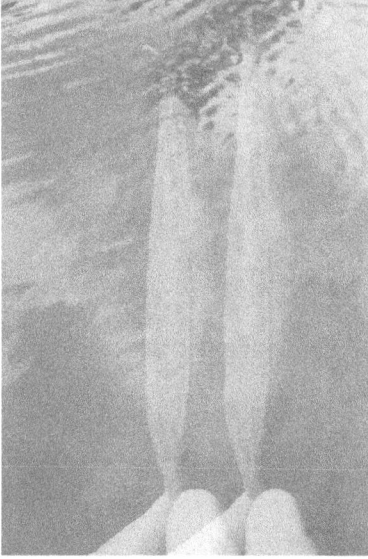
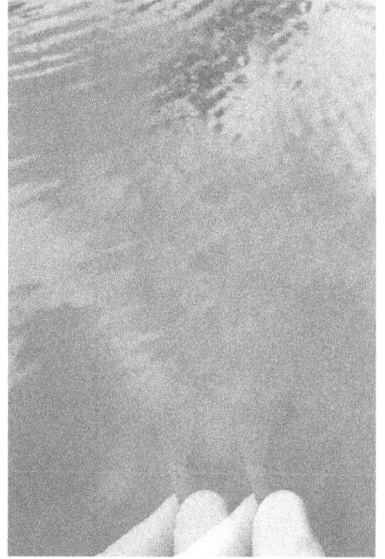

I was having fun shifting my perception and viewing real-life objects in ways they don't ordinarily appear to us. It was freeing my mind like I never imagined before. The interplay of form and formlessness, light and illusion was stimulating my imagination and I was becoming more creative about all kinds of possible experiments I could do. Once it occurred to me that I should look at two similar objects simultaneously. So I took a plumeria flower in each hand and brought them close together. As I applied my visual technique, a third flower appeared in the middle as a combined replica of the other two. It created the effect of a virtual flower becoming manifest.

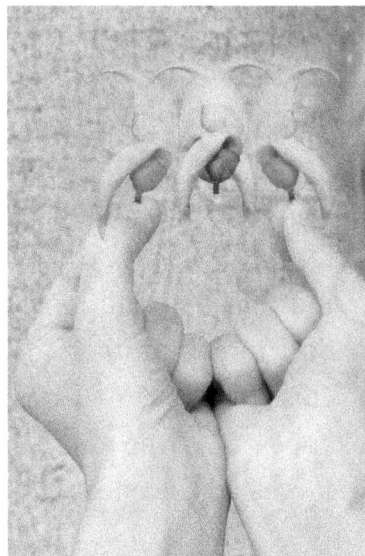

I also enjoyed going to the beach and practicing with a beautiful blue sky as my meditation background. I even experimented at nighttime, pointing my hands or other objects toward the moon. My eyes became like a photographic lens taking thousands of snapshots of solid objects appearing in a translucent mode. Over time, I mastered this visual process and so began to grasp a deeper message through these practices. I came to understand more clearly the relationship between spirit and matter, and the role that our perception plays in creating the experience of living in the material world. It was changing the hard-wiring in my brain and permanently transforming my worldview.

I was taking notes about my discoveries, thoughts and observations, and the number of pages was growing daily. It became a study, a spiritual investigation into the realm of spirit and perception. With every new discovery I felt even more inspired and motivated to continue. I had a keen sense of higher purpose unfolding right before my eyes.

One day I came across a fascinating book, *The Holographic Universe* by Michael Talbot, in which he discussed thought provoking concepts and ideas about the holographic nature of our universe. According to this theory, the universe is a giant moving hologram made out of light waves. They are continually passing through each other and overlapping into arrays of geometric light patterns. Our brain and vision function like a holographic lens converting these light patterns into a 3-D reality. In other words, our brains create a virtual reality which we perceive as a physical world. I realized that the holographic theory was essentially implying the same truth as, for example, Buddha's teaching of emptiness. Both the scientific and the metaphysical approaches conveyed in their own unique way the notion of illusion. Each proposed that even though the material world appears to be solid, there is an underlying non-material aspect to it that is hidden from our "normal" perception. Our senses co-create the physical aspect, while simultaneously veiling the original source, which is the living matrix of light.

Reading Michael's book was like finding the missing peace of my puzzle. It facilitated a quantum leap in consciousness, opening my mind to a holographic level of thinking. I realized that there was a meaningful connection between this theory and my project. I saw an original parallel between my visual technique and the holographic worldview. That inspired me to name it holographic gazing or simply "Hologazing".

By shifting my ordinary perception into "holo-mode", I could observe the principles of the holographic universe right through my hands, the macrocosm at a microcosmic scale. Seeing through rocks and leaves, or observing virtual flowers emerging out of the void are mind-expanding visual metaphors. Instead of thinking and reading complex scientific explanations, I could simply hologaze and meditate on the imagery, assimilating the deeper understanding intuitively. Hologazing was quickly reeducating my perception of reality and helping me to shift the paradigm from mechanistic/materialistic to quantum/holographic. Before, in my normal mode of perception, I was interacting with reality as a conglomeration of solid separate forms out there. By Hologazing, I could see through the illusion of these forms, understanding the separation and duality they create.

When I first discovered Hologazing, I was curious to find out more about the nature of the visual effects. Later on I realized that through regular practice my ability to concentrate was dramatically improving. Engaging in this process was like flexing my mind's muscles on an invisible exercise machine. It involved both my hands and eyes, demanding undivided attention. I was totally transfixed by the all-absorbing, ethereal quality of these transparent geometric hand patterns.

Prolonged gazing often induced profound altered states of consciousness. At the point of achieving complete concentration, my mind would shift to yet another level. At these moments of finest alignment a sensation of weightlessness would arise in me. Any feeling of density would disappear from my body and I felt suspended beyond gravity, floating within my inner expanded space. Feeling almost breathless and motionless, I became immersed in a profound stillness of being. It was amazing how long I could hold the hand positions up in the air without my arms getting tired. It felt as if some magnetic force was effortlessly supporting them.

While in these states of lucid waking, I was merging with what I can only describe as "The All". The sharp outlines of the outer world would dissolve and assume a milky, sublime quality. Nothing appeared really solid or static. The separation between inside and outside melted away as I experienced a total fusion of these paradoxical environments. I could merge into a unified field of light both in and all around me. Such mystical experiences were gradually transforming my relationship to everything that meant spiritual to me, and the word physical no longer had the same meaning as before.

Hologazing was like a secret door opening into infinity. It was the bridge between body and mind, the conscious and super-conscious realms. I began using it with the intent to merge and communicate with the divine source. Shifting perception with my physical eyes opened my inner eye, inducing deep meditation which connected me to the invisible domain of spirit. It was awakening me to a more intimate, deeper experience of universal Oneness. I realized what a profound influence our perception exerts on our attitude and philosophy of life. Coincidentally, as I was able to shift my perception, everything else shifted as well. Seeing everything as an extension of my being, I felt more attuned with the whole universe and all living beings. It was much easier for me to access a deep inner feeling of unity. The privilege of such experiences was a major breakthrough in my spiritual evolution.

At the same time, the hand symbols provided me with a model, a systematic approach to my personal growth. They were essential to focusing my intention. Instead of wasting my mental energy, I now had tools to concentrate my mind on them. Whenever I experienced conflict or duality, whenever I needed to heal myself or change my life, I would reach out to these divine tools for help. They were like mystic master keys, opening the inner door to my true self and the freedom that lies within. Meditating with them had a comforting, soothing effect on me. I felt protected by them. They seemed to have an almost mystical, wish-fulfilling quality, removing obstacles from my path. I noticed the more I practiced and the stronger my intention, the faster the results.

I also realized that a right inner attitude played an important role. I valued my lotus hands as sacred spiritual tools and used them as such. Before practicing, I washed and anointed them with aroma oils. Through their use breakthroughs were more readily available when the situation called for it, and I was able to effectively integrate them into everyday life. I was beginning to realize my transformation was real and substantial.

For a time I didn't understand the meaning of the hand symbols. They were like abstract hieroglyphs to me and I attempted to decode them through constant inquiry. It was up to me and my level of commitment to persist through whatever challenges arose. Since I had no one to ask, I had to look inside for answers. I had to develop laser concentration and sharp intuition, a process which took years of deep contemplation.

The evolutionary process from abstract forms to meaningful symbols fascinated me. Specific hand poses were related to kindred life themes. They would appear over and over as if by divine orchestration. Jung called this phenomenon *synchronicity*. I learned to pay attention to such "coincidences" and became more confident in assigning meaning to a particular pattern. This was incredibly confirming to me that I was on the right path.

Finally, after years of inquiry I was able to put the pieces of the puzzle together. However, I had so many questions it was essential to develop patience and persistence. Answers always seemed to come after an incubation period as if they first needed to ripen in the subconscious. I never tried to define things with my intellect. I really wanted to learn the Truth of all this, and knew it could only come directly from the source. Everything in the universe exists as patterns of light, and our brains are the receivers and transmitters which resonate with those patterns of information. I felt my mind was like a tuning fork, receiving information telepathically. Through the hand forms, the transference of information seemed to go through a step-down process from the source to the physical to the symbolism.

Over time, a new 21st Century generation of archetypal hand symbols was born. They express deeply ingrained spiritual truths we all share, such as Oneness, Love and Compassion. Jung emphasized the importance of universal symbols and archetypes. Through them man communicates with the realm of the psyche, which is so important to psychological well-being. Meditation enables our mind to enter the collective unconscious and achieve wholeness through that connection.

The hand patterns are a new symbolism of the sacred. They are primal shapes that reflect the root of creation as patterns of light. As symbols of wholeness they heal the body-mind separation and lead to psychic growth. As hand mandalas they are representations of order and unity and are conducive to the achievement of balance and harmony.

This is how I discovered and created the healing art of Akash Khi. Looking back at this amazing evolutionary journey, I realize that it was all right there in my hands! They are simple enough for anyone to do, yet as with all archetypes these hand mudras hold within them the wisdom of creation. For me, and I hope for you, they are sacred.

"All our knowledge is the offspring of our perceptions."

- Leonardo da Vinci

Uncovering The Nature Of Reality

All Life Is Made Of The Same "Thing"

The science of cosmology estimates our universe was born approximately fifteen billion years ago. All the matter which the observable universe contains today was originally concentrated into an infinitely dense pinpoint of energy. Due to tremendous compression generating trillions of degrees of heat it erupted in a titanic explosion of light commonly known as the "Big Bang" theory.[1] In those initial stages the baby universe was made totally of light, and had no distinct features. Continuing to expand and shape itself through various stages of evolution, millions of galaxies, stars and planets gradually emerged, spreading out into the vast cosmic regions.

The primal division of cosmic Oneness began with the separation between light and matter. Visible matter mysteriously began forming from this unified field with the emergence of the first subatomic particles, called quarks.[2] As they joined together to form protons, neutrons and electrons, the first elements of hydrogen and helium were created. The further combining and recombining of these basic subatomic particles evolved into the Periodic Table of Elements as we know it today. These 118 elements represent the building blocks of reality. As we can see, over millenniums all organic and inorganic matter was created through an intelligent process on this cosmic assembly line.

An amazing example of this shuffling and reshuffling process are the countless different species on our planet today. They came into existence through endless variations in the sequence of just four genetic letters: A, T, G and C. The basic structure of DNA is built out of adenine, thymine, guanine and cytosine.[3] A, T, G, and C are the four letters of the DNA genetic code, providing information for the assembly of the species. Although DNA varies from one species to another, the four basic components are the same. Thus, there is no fundamental division between humans and all other species. Based on our DNA make-up we are all genetically related. Our uniqueness as human beings results solely from the modifications of a universally shared genetic code.

Judging by external characteristics we appear to be radically different from most other living beings. While there seems to be little in common between a human being, a butterfly, a rose, a dolphin or an eagle, looks can be deceptive. Despite these external differences we are more greatly interconnected than meets the eye. Scientific research of fossil deposits proves we are related to each other through one common ancestor. Every person, every animal and plant, every visible and invisible lifeform, originates from a tiny bacterium. This single-celled organism can be traced as far back as an estimated 3.8 billion years ago. It represents the very root of universal Oneness that continued to branch out into an impressive "Tree of Life".[4] Today, there are more than three million different species inhabiting the Earth, with humans, so far, as the crown of creation in a long chain of life.

What about the differentiation between organic and inorganic life? To think that there is no fundamental distinction between these categories is a big stretch in logic, yet scientists say there is no sharp division between living and non-living things. There is no fundamental difference between a carbon atom in our body, in a diamond, or in a piece of coal. Bohm's scientific theory of Undivided Wholeness states that life, matter and consciousness are essentially different projections from the same Source.[5]

As we continue our inquiry into the true nature of reality, the common thread of universal Oneness remains unbroken no matter what aspect of creation we examine. Exploring the subatomic realms of visible matter enabled scientists to further unravel the mysteries of creation and the principle of unity. When we look at our external world we see so much variety - people, plants, animals, planets, galaxies and so forth. But regardless of this diversity, the material world is uniform at the ground level. External differences between rocks, threes, flowers or any other created thing completely disappear.

Underlying form is an invisible network of energy frequencies and their interconnections. The unbroken continuum of all subatomic processes is a manifestation of unity we can call the Oneness of all life, our true nature. Creation, no matter how diversified, is actually the "flesh of God" in many physical disguises. All is made of the same thing.

In ancient times, through deep spiritual inquiry, the idea of Oneness was born in the minds of sages and mystics. They spoke of this with an irrevocable sense of knowing and confidence, even though at that time there was no scientific evidence available to verify their insights. Thousands of years later, with the scientific confirmation we have at hand now, such profound accuracy of intuitive perception appears nothing less than miraculous. In fact, the concept of Oneness formed the foundations of the world's great religions.

In Hinduism the ultimate reality is called Brahman, the cosmic Spirit. Indian Rishis referred to Oneness as the womb of all things, or the navel of the universe.[6] The Buddhist uses the term Dharma-Kaya (Body of Being) to express the same idea.[7] In the Chinese tradition we come across the concept of Tao.[8] In Western religions the principle of Oneness is conveyed through the exclusive adoration of one central deity - Yahweh, Allah, Christ. Various paths, one truth. Despite any theological differences, most spiritual traditions share the common truth of universal Oneness.

Grasping the complexities of the true nature of reality is obviously not an easy task. The idea of Oneness is rather abstract and difficult to integrate into our daily lives. In fact, our five senses are continually assuring us that we are separate. It's hard to recognize the sameness between our hot sun millions of miles away and frozen icebergs at the North Pole. What about the sameness between living beings and dead objects? Such paradoxical extremes are rather difficult to consider as a unified whole. However, we now know that separation is an illusion. The ultimate reality is just one super-consciousness playing itself out in a multitude of forms and roles, with everything originating from the same source. This is universal Oneness.

We Are Beings Of Light

Things become even more intriguing and controversial as we come across the idea that the solidity of physical matter is basically an illusion. Contrary to our normal perception scientific research indicates that more than ninety-nine percent of our familiar solid world, including all living creatures, consists of empty space. Atoms that make up solid matter are extremely small, consisting almost entirely of a vacuum. Practically all of an atom's mass is contained within a tiny nucleus one one-hundred-thousandth times smaller than the atom itself. "To see the nucleus, we would have to blow up the atom to the size of the largest dome in the world, the dome of St Peter's Cathedral in Rome. In an atom of that size, the nucleus would be the size of a grain of salt!"[9] Theoretically speaking, "If the whole human body were compressed to its nuclear density it would not take up more space than a pinhead."[10]

Then what gives matter its familiar solid appearance? The theoretical physicist Fritjof Capra describes the solidity of matter as a consequence of the so-called quantum effect. High velocities in the atom give our world solid appearance.

"In the atom, now, there are two competing forces. On the

one hand, the electrons are bound to the nucleus by electric forces which try to keep them as close as possible. On the other hand, they respond to their confinement by whirling around, and the tighter they are bound to the nucleus, the higher velocity will be. The confinement of electrons in an atom results in enormous velocities of about 600 miles per second. These high velocities make the atom appear as a rigid sphere, just as a fast rotating propeller appears as a disc."[11]

The recent invention of laser beams and three-dimensional holograms have ignited yet another scientific revolution - providing a key to the Holographic Theory of Reality. This new perspective confirms that the whole universe is fundamentally empty, a giant kaleidoscopic hologram of light. Scientific evidence suggests that our world and everything in it are holographic images, projections of light from a reality beyond our own. Though we are human holograms living in this holographic matrix of light, the great paradox is that our experience of feeling hot or cold and pain or pleasure, for example, are nevertheless very real.

Just like the progressive ideas of Copernicus, Galileo and Newton shattered the accepted theories of their day, this model of the Universe is transforming our present worldview. The main architects of this theory are David Bohm and Karl Pribram. Bohm, a former protégé of Einstein, is one of the world's most respected quantum physicists. Pribram is a neurophysiologist at Stanford University and author of *Languages of the Brain*. Working independently of one another, both scientists came to similar conclusions which led them to the formulation of this groundbreaking theory. This theory of reality is shifting our paradigm from materialistic/mechanistic to quantum/holographic.

If we accept what the scientists are saying, then who in fact are we? Are we human holograms, phantoms of light living in a virtual 3-D cosmic show without even realizing it? Have you ever seen a 3-D movie? In order to achieve the illusion of virtual imagery you need special glasses. What we see is just a stream of frequencies coming from the projector translated into 3-D. We can use this as an example of how the holographic universe functions. We don't need 3-D glasses because our eyes already have holographic properties built into them. According to this model we are participants in a colossal 3-D movie we call Life.

Eyes are sophisticated sensors equipped with holographic lenses that visually create the experience of material reality. They have a "special-effects" filter to convert light waves into three-dimensional images. Scientific experiments are leading to the belief that our other senses - taste, touch, hearing and smell - also have holographic properties. They analyze and convert wave-like frequencies through their own task-specific filters. When our five senses are combined together they create an extremely believable experience of living in the material world.

Living In The Holographic Universe

Since the invention of holograms inspired the birth of the holographic theory, let us take a closer look at them - what they are and how they are created. In comparison to material sculptures a hologram is a 3-D light sculpture. It looks just like a solid real object - a vase for example - but if you try touching it your hand will pass right through it, as though it's moving through empty space.

The first hologram was invented by Dr. Dennis Gabor, a researcher at the Imperial College in London. He was able to record images holographically, but they weren't clear because he was using white light which is incoherent (traveling in different frequencies at different phases). Lasers give us a much better production of holograms because they are pure light, that is, coherent, focused, and traveling in the same frequency and phase.

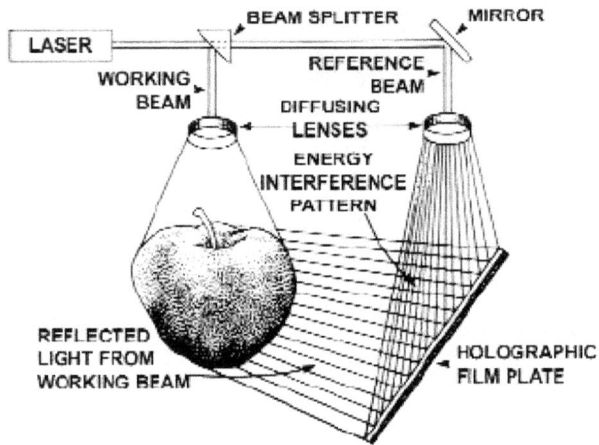

To create a hologram, a photographic image is taken of an object. Reflected from the object, a single laser beam is split into two beams. When both beams crisscross and pass through each other, they create intricate wave patterns called interference patterns. When a bright light source is shone through them, the photographed image appears in three-dimensional form. Such a holographic sculpture is purely an optical illusion, a virtual 3-D image concocted from light waves. Even though it looks real, it is fundamentally nonexistent.[12]

Holograms demonstrate how invisible light waves become real looking three-dimensional images via interference patterns. Our entire universe is flooded with a variety of waves invisible to the human eye - light waves, radio waves, X-rays and gamma rays. They are constantly crisscrossing and creating these interference patterns. Our holographic brain has the ability to analyze and convert wave patterns into real-life experiences and familiar images.

As mentioned earlier, our vision is holographic. The process of image recognition in our eyes is called stereoscopic vision.[13] If you look at an object with first one eye shut and then the other, you will find that the image seen by each eye differs slightly. Assessing those differences and computing the depth and the position of external objects in space, our brain builds three-dimensional images by overlapping the views coming from the left and the right eye to the retinas. It literally fuses them into a single image.

This whole process, from perception to recognition of objects, takes place in the form of light signals. When light beams bounce off external objects, they enter the eyes through the pupil and strike hundreds of millions of photo-detectors inside the curved surface of the eyeball. This information travels through the network of optical nerves to the brain for processing.

Our material world looks concrete because the brain converts random waves into concrete images. Scientists are not saying solid objects don't exist. Rather they are made from light that manifests itself as form. For example, when an image of a flower is filtered through the holographic lens of the brain it appears as a real flower. But if we were to bypass the lens we would experience it purely as a light pattern. What is real, and what is illusion?[14]

According to Pribram our brains are capable of creating internal three-dimensional holograms. The extremities of the brain's nerve cells look like tree branches tightly positioned next to each other. When electrical nerve currents pass through them they radiate outward in a wave-like motion. Then they create expanding ripples of electricity that criss-cross and form interference patterns, giving rise to internal three-dimensional forms. He further ascertains it is these expanding ripples creating interference patterns that produce the holographic properties of the brain.[15] Thus our brain constructs internal holograms projected outward as 3-D reality.

Three-dimensionality is not the only extraordinary characteristic of the hologram. Another thought-provoking feature is that it's indivisible. If you cut it into many pieces each piece still contains the complete image. This tells us that our individual identities are inseparable from the whole, that we are actually an extension of a universal energy field. Beyond the visible surface each of us is like a complex web of interference patterns between people, nature and the cosmos.

The holographic matrix is the storehouse of all information. Science, medicine, philosophy, spirituality and in fact all knowledge come from this source. Our individual consciousness is embedded in this information field since the beginning of time. We all hold information of everyone and everything, whether we're aware of it or not. In deep meditation we can tap into this vast reservoir of knowledge.

That our minds are all interconnected explains the phenomena of telepathy and synchronicity. Since every thought and action creates a ripple effect, by uniting our minds around the same idea - for example Oneness - we could ignite a mass shift in consciousness. Any events that happen to or around us are universally encoded, so living in this shared reality we can improve the world by simply improving our own life. We can contribute to the healing of all by interacting in more loving, compassionate ways.

The Yin And Yang Of Creation

I am particles, I am waves. I am solid, I am empty. I am a holographic energy field, but also my material body. Exploring the nature of reality, we have learned it has two sides: Spirit and Matter. They are diametrically opposed but not mutually exclusive, a paradox not easily reconciled logically. They both make up the continuum of Oneness. Scientists have discovered that light itself exists in a dual mode - as waves and particles. This "wave-particle duality" is one of the most important concepts in quantum physics. It is known as Bohr's Complementarity Principle.[16]

Experiments have further demonstrated that it is impossible to observe both simultaneously. Depending on how scientists set up their measuring devices, they can see either the particle or the wave aspect of matter, but never both at the same time. Yet only if the two are joined together do we get a complete picture. According to Heisenberg's Uncertainty Principle[17] this is not related to the limitations of experimental measuring apparatus. So reality has two profiles but one face. Evidently Mother Nature is willing to show us only one side of her face at a time!

Consciousness is the foundation of reality and itself has a dual nature. It exists as unlimited formless consciousness and the limited particularized consciousness, which creates reality by morphing into wave patterns. The wave aspect is the implicate order, the particle aspect is the explicate order. The seen and the unseen coexist simultaneously. The inner reality being projected outward is a perceptual phenomenon. Consciousness realizes its true nature by self-reflection and observation. It is the "Eye of God" looking at itself.

The principle of complementarity is a universal law. Light-dark, male-female, body-mind, and particle-antiparticle are all examples of the infinite spectrum of polar opposites which comprise the fabric of the universe. This phenomenon can be observed throughout multiple dimensions, from galactic proportions all the way down to the infinitely small subatomic world. It is exalted in Eastern mysticism, with Shiva/Shakti and Yin/Yang being two of its more well known spiritual concepts.

Nature pulsates in rhythmic oscillations between her poles. It is the eternal heartbeat of creation; it perpetuates motion and life but also holds the universe together in a state of perfect equilibrium. Complementing each other, polar opposites exist in a dynamic state of balance. The middle line of symmetry between the poles represents the cosmic axis of nature. Balance is a cosmic law of survival.

If, for example, the Earth moved closer or further away from the sun, life on our planet would be destroyed due to extreme heat or cold. If forces inside atoms became unbalanced, they would either violently collapse inward or be blown apart.

As a part of Nature we are no exception. We resonate in harmony with her rhythms when we are able to maintain balance.

Finding the golden mean between spirit and matter is essential to our wholeness. It's the balance between waking and sleeping, doing and being, selfishness and selflessness. Focusing on sensory pleasures and acquiring material possessions while neglecting or negating spiritual values is one extreme. Choosing material poverty, false humility and self-abnegation for the purpose of spiritual achievements is another. Sidhharta Gauthama was born a prince into a royal family and raised in opulence. After he left home, he became an ascetic, embracing detachment from material possessions. Upon his awakening he became the Buddha, teaching the Middle Way between material fullness and spiritual emptiness. True freedom lies in the sense of proportion between spiritual and materialistic goals and values in life.

Awakening The Mind

Thousands of years ago, when there was no applicable scientific knowledge, it was the role of spiritual traditions to teach us about the nature of reality. They fulfilled this task through an intuitive approach using symbols and metaphoric narration. Ordinary language was considered too limited to express their teachings. During the last hundred years modern science has provided us with cutting edge paradigmshifting theories and insights into the true nature of reality. The revolutionary hi-tech experiments such as bombing atoms in gigantic particle colliders enabled scientists to probe into the deepest core of matter, further enlightening us about the mysterious workings of creation. Though very different approaches, science and spirituality converge in their outlook on reality, ultimately arriving at the same conclusion.

Modern science describes physical reality as a holographic grand illusion. In most spiritual teachings the concept of illusion plays a very significant role. Maya (the veil of illusion) is a Sanskrit term that translates as "that which does not exist". It represents multiplicity, the tangible world of appearances. It is the illusory sense of separation, of ego, you and me, yours and mine.

A magician's tricks exemplify how we are fooled into believing what is not real. We co-create an illusion by misperception and false conclusions. The material world is like a magic show in which we participate. The effects of three-dimensionality and solidity of matter are so profoundly genuine, we are easily mislead into believing that what we see, taste or touch, is "real" in a material sense. This dream we call reality is so flawless that it's very difficult to see through the illusion. Every living creature succumbs to it naturally, as if under a collective hypnosis. Without realizing it, all our thoughts, actions and desires are conditioned by this phenomenon. Our illusions are only destroyed through true knowledge.

The seduction of the senses is an extremely powerful force, yet without it the earthly plane would lose its allure. We feel alive through sense stimulation and the pleasures derived from images, sounds, smells, tastes and tactile sensations. How else would it be possible for us to enjoy life if it weren't tangible and concrete in the dimensions of time and space? Isn't the experience of living in the material world undeniably a marvel of our Spirit's creative genius? If you see through the holographic effects, the lights come on in this 3-D cinema of life, and the show is over!

It's not the physical experience, but rather a lack of understanding that is the main obstacle to happiness and well-being. The issue is overly identifying with the physical aspect, a one-sided perception that leads to a predominantly materialistic view of life. Such a limited belief system is one of the chief causes of suffering. Bridging the paradoxical aspects of nature into a unified worldview will engender spiritual values of peace, balance and harmony in our lives. But unless we are willing to awaken the mind, materialistic and egotistical attitudes will prevail. Healing will only be attained by embracing our true nature of universal Oneness. With this inquiry we begin our journey of transformation.

"What happens when people open their hearts?
They get better."

- Haruki Murakami

Healing The Separation Syndrome

The Root of Suffering

At birth our umbilical cord is cut off, symbolizing the primal division between spirit and matter. We are disunited not only from our earthly mother, but also from our spiritual source of Oneness. As soon as we emerge from the birth canal our identification with the physical begins, and we start to become aware of self and other. We begin the shift from unity into duality. For a moment imagine shutting off all your senses, including your mind. You would instantly merge back into a state of undifferentiated Oneness. Switch the senses on again, and you are back in the body.

Existence in the world of form implies a division between the observer and the observed. Without the experiencer: You - and the experienced: The world - there is no experience. While separation is necessary so we can form relationships and participate in the beauty of diversity, there is also a downside to it. Like positive and negative, light and dark, it's a two-sided coin. The sense of separation can bring us together, but it can also pull us apart and cause us a great deal of suffering.

Some suffering, such as the painfulness of giving birth, is part of nature and cannot be avoided. The sad thing is that most of our suffering is self-created, and could be avoided.

Due to our ignorance, we cause each other a lot of unnecessary harm. We fall into the trap of dualistic thinking which tends to divide and categorize things as good or bad, desirable or undesirable. This perspective often results in seeing others as rivals in the drive for self-gratification.

The me-versus-you vantage point creates the stage for survival struggles and ego battles. Like a domino effect it spreads into violence, envy and jealousy. It provokes antagonistic forces which diminish our happiness and well-being. We all see many examples of suffering fueled by our ego-driven pursuits. Some of us will lie, steal, or cheat in an effort to increase our own self-worth at the expense of others. Hubris and the drive for power often end up as a rationale for tyranny and corruption. Wars and the destruction of life are tragic examples of the negative power of separation and human ignorance.

That we exist independently from one another is true on a physical level. But holographically speaking, separation is relative. Two islands look separate, but below the water they are part of the same earth. In the same way, we are interconnected through a unified field. From a broader perspective we could say that deceiving another is also an act of self-deception, or that harming another is the same as harming ourselves. If someone's happiness makes us sad, or someone's sadness makes us happy, we are functioning from a disconnected space in our consciousness. Because everyone is an extension of our own energy field, being at war with others is like being at war with ourselves.

The forces of separation harm and disconnect us not only from others, but from our own self. The holographic matrix exerts a powerful influence over our mind and imagination. We are easily seduced by this three-dimensional reality with visions of money, power, status and worldly pleasures. If we are not careful as we strive to attain those things, the matrix can spin a web around us. Maya, the force of illusion, draws us outward like a turtle from its shell, gradually entangling us more and more and distracting us from what really matters. When material values take precedence over spiritual ones, we can become alienated from our true nature and purpose.

Separation implies a loss of balance, whereby one side predominates at the expense of the other. This tilted worldview is reflected in all areas of our life. In order to heal ourselves we need to let go of one-sided attachments and learn to honor the balance between personal interests and those of others. By restoring the equilibrium between our spiritual and material needs, greater happiness in life will surely follow.

No matter what the suffering, at the core it is usually some form of conflict in duality. The multitude of problems that plague us individually and collectively are not random, they are fundamentally interrelated. They are all apples from the same tree. These negative phenomena are the signs and symptoms of a universal spiritual disease - the Separation Syndrome.

Finding Balance

The Separation Syndrome is not easily overcome. We must target where it originates, in our five senses - especially eyesight. First we see things, then we interpret what we see. Sight is a faculty of awareness far more basic than the intellect. Our eyesight has been evolving for billions of years, much earlier than intellect and language. On a second-to-second basis our thoughts are being molded by our vision, influencing our attitudes, behaviors and actions.

Like a cascading effect, vision initiates a chain reaction that translates into every aspect of our life. Physical, emotional or mental imbalance can be traced back to our perception. Change your thoughts - change your life, that is true. Since seeing precedes thinking, we must go one step back. Change your perception - change your thoughts - change your life. In other words, we must first reconcile our basic outlook. Correcting the imbalances in our reasoning and doing leads to a more balanced worldview, to a more peaceful and harmonious life.

Transforming our perception of reality is of course easier said than done. We see what we see, and what we see is an incredibly believable material world. Under normal circumstances it's impossible to see this as illusory. We need to be aware that our universe is a holographic light projection of cosmic proportions. We are in it, connected from the inside out through the gateway of our holographic eyes. And if the holographic super-construct were too easy to see through, we wouldn't so easily enjoy the beauty of our physical nature.

Imagine the tree in your backyard randomly appearing and disappearing due to "technical difficulties" in the internal holographic matrix programming. Or what if the apple you are about to eat suddenly becomes a translucent hologram, and your hand goes right through it? If the appearance of our physical world was that inconsistent, we would more easily wake up to its illusion. Instead, we are bound by our perception of the holographic mirage because it seems to be the path of lesser resistance. Based on what we see, almost by default, we prescribe to a materialistic belief system. Then, separation is an inevitable.

This is the great challenge with our perception. It is difficult to shift, because visual impressions have been crystallizing since birth into materialistically colored images of "reality". The eye is a lens of perception similar to a camera, constantly taking snapshots of the world around us. In our lifetime we record billions upon billions of visual impressions. Our eyes are the entry point of almost all the information we take in. Of the three billion messages relayed to the brain every second, two billion are sent from the eye. They are encrusted into layered images of the material reality - hard to change. They are the key instruments through which we learn about the world we live in. The information we obtain visually leave neuronal traces in the brain. They become deeply etched into our subconscious, dominating the intellect and shaping our worldview.

The question is how can we shift our perception of reality if our vision is set on 3-D mode? This limited perception constantly reinforces only the material side of nature and thus our sense of separation. But imagine if we could see through solid objects and view them as waves of energy patterns, as holograms of light. That would certainly restore the balance between spirit and matter by reinforcing the non-material side of nature. Hologazing can be the missing link to the wholeness we are looking for.

Hologazing is sort of like "X-ray vision" - a meditation done with open eyes gazing at things in a way that shifts our perception of them. For example, we normally see a leaf as a solid separate object, but with the help of Hologazing the leaf looks transparent. This effect creates a breakthrough in awareness. Here we actually use our eyes to show us the opposite of form, to unveil the formlessness of things. This tricks the brain into reinterpreting and redefining our view and our belief about the leaf. Seeing both the material and non-material aspect of things gives us a balanced perspective.

In order to eliminate the suffering in ourselves and the world caused by the Separation Syndrome, we propose a 'holographic approach' - introducing a signature Hologazing Meditation Technique. This is the visual path that takes us on an enlightening journey. It presupposes that if we can change how we see, our thoughts and beliefs will change as well.

Hologazing is more than just a technique, it signifies a state of mind. Seeing through matter as if we had X-ray vision symbolizes the opening of our spiritual eye, and then we are able to pierce through the veils of Maya and dissolve the illusions which obscure the Truth.

Our mind was not always capable of perceiving the full spectrum of colors. In the early stages of our evolution we only saw red and black. Later, perception of other colors slowly emerged. Color sense is just one example of the gradual evolution of consciousness. This means that when a concept is born within the mind, it becomes manifest. Hologazing as a new perceptual skill represents a step forward in the evolution of consciousness.

The Hologazing Meditation

Hologazing is a coined expression combining holographic and gazing. Holographic presents the idea of the world as a hologram of light while gazing suggests a philosophic contemplation, a visual meditation on the nature of reality. Hologazing in its higher sense means to see clearly and know directly how something is. It signifies an insight beyond the surface, a direct witnessing of our true nature.

As a visual technique Hologazing is dynamically similar to those of a photographic lens zooming in and out. Our pupils function like a camera lens operated by the brain and the eye muscles. In order to avoid blurry images, it focuses light entering the retina with great precision. Normally our eyes zoom onto a selected object. So in order to switch to hologazing mode we make them see beyond the object, into the distance. Our perception changes dramatically by simply adjusting the zoom lens within the eye.

Hologazing can be described as looking at close up objects while the lens of the eyes is set to a distant viewing mode. In other words, you bring an object up to your eyes as if you want to examine it very closely, but instead you gaze through it. Because the object is so close to your eyes you are still looking at it, but only indirectly. Then the selected object changes form and its holographic imagery starts emerging right before your eyes. Right there a rare window of opportunity opens up and Nature begins to unveil some of her innermost secrets!

As an awakening technique, Hologazing introduces two key visual effects designed to ignite perceptual breakthroughs: The Wave-Particle Effect and The Holographic Effect. They elicit powerful spiritual symbolism that appeals to our intuitive mind. These mind-expanding visuals enable us to look at familiar objects from the holographic vantage point, changing how we view ourselves and the world around us. Simply put, Hologazing is a meditative process which dissolves the body-mind separation. Through regular practice we develop holographic awareness and a sense of harmony.

The more we practice, the deeper the transformation. It is not enough to try it once or twice and just get it on an intellectual level. This is a gradual process, and the visuals must sink deep into the unconscious. It is not something which ordinarily happens overnight. The subtle impressions subliminally change the hard-wiring of the brain. Just like charging an empty battery, we must saturate our mind with this virtual imagery. Hologazing works on an intuitive level, beyond the trappings of temporal thought.

In the following series of Hologazing Exercises we begin to awaken step by step. Each meditation shifts our normal perception in order to view solid objects in ways they don't ordinarily appear to us. Each visual effect propels us into an intuitive mode, triggering flashes of insight and deepening our understanding. Practitioners experience "aha" moments, freeing their perception from limitations imposed by the logical mind. These exercises should not be viewed separately, but as stages of inquiry. They are integral steps toward self-realization wich unveil the holographic secrets of our consciousness.

The Wave-Particle Exercises

Step One

Hold one hand vertically with the palm sideways directly between your eyes, approximately 10 inches away from your face.

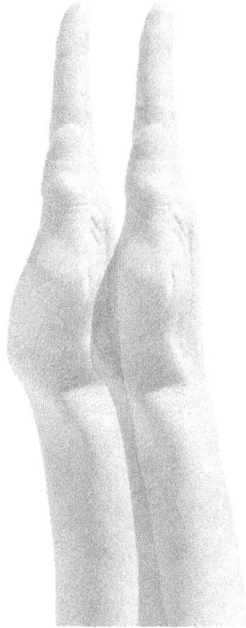

Step Two

Now apply Hologazing. With the hand in the same position, shift your focus and look through your hand into the distance. Witness the doubling effect of the hand as well as its assuming a transparent, wave-like appearance. I recommend a white wall, a plain background, or even the open sky to best observe this visual imagery.

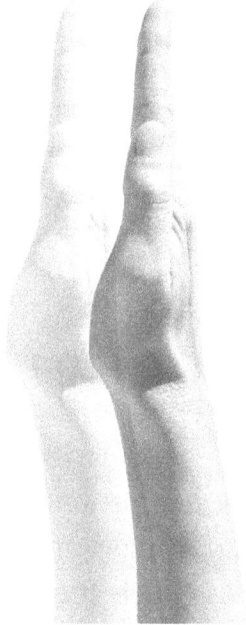

Step Three

Continue gazing steadily through your hand for several minutes. Observe the appearance of a double hand oscillating back and forth, sometimes appearing to be solid, sometimes transparent, and at times completely vanishing!

Commentary

Reality is dual in nature, composed of light which appears both as waves and particles. The Wave-Particle Meditation Exercise introduces an effect whereby our hand alternates between solid and transparent appearance. The imagery parallels the wave-particle duality inherent in nature. By connecting us to both simultaneously, this meditation heals the spirit/matter separation.

In this exercise we are exploring what happens to our hand when viewed in holo-mode. It becomes a double image, a transparent layer between form and formlessness through which we can see the background. Normally images from both eyes are fused into a single one, but here we are observing the reverse process, in which the hand transforms into two independent, transparent images.

As we continue, we observe another unusual phenomenon: The double phantom hand is transparent until it completely vanishes for a moment, then reappears. This yin-yang, wave-particle dance continues for as long as we are in holo-mode. This imagery provides a simple yet powerful analogy for the scientific concept of wave-particle duality. The physical hand appears sometimes as a particle picture and sometimes as a wave picture, rhythmically oscillating back and forth between the two. Practicing this simple meditation reprograms us. It deepens our awareness of the material and immaterial, the visible and invisible aspects of reality that coexist and complement each other.

If we move our eyes around while keeping the hand in a steady position, the visual effect remains intact. Even if we move the hand slowly to the left or right across the face, we still see the background through the hand. Normally we would expect it to obscure the background, but in this case the transparent images are not caused by the crossing of the eyes or in some other unnatural way, but by simply changing the focus.

This is the question: Is our hand really solid or just a phantom image which our mind perceives as such? Our role as observer is of fundamental importance. Depending on whether we look at the hand directly or indirectly, it alternates from a solid to a wave-like image. When we look at our hand directly it appears solid, but when we hologaze, it dissolves as though it were empty. So, which one is real and which is an illusion? This exercise demonstrates that what we perceive as the outside world is not the absolute truth. Our interpretation of reality is relative, dependent on our mode of perception.

Practice Guidelines

Before starting this exercise, select about a dozen of different objects that you will hologaze at as your meditation instruments. In order to best see the wave-particle effect, these particular objects should not be wider than two inches. If we were giants and the distance between our eyes much greater, then we could hologaze through cars, trees, buildings. But since the distance between our eyes is rather small, we have to practice with small objects. For example: a narrow leaf, a pencil, a banana, a cell phone, silverware or other objects of your choice. Of course, you can always use your hand as a basic wave-particle meditation instrument. The advantage of using the hand is that it is always there, no props are necessary. Wherever you are, you can easily engage in Hologazing through your hand.

You can practice in a sitting or standing position. Hold your hand or the selected object as previously described. If you are having difficulty seeing the wave-particle effect, focus on another object or surface in the background. Breathe slowly and relax your eyes until the effect arises. Try to practice in daylight so you can see very clearly. Pay attention to all the subtle nuances that reveal themselves in this process of visual self-discovery. Play with different objects and allow yourself to be surprised again and again. The information that the mind computes is deeply subliminal. It is more lasting and profoundly transformational than our intellectual understanding.

Move a selected object very slowly across your face, to the

left and right. Contrary to your expectation, the object doesn't obstruct anything. You can see the total background at all times. Practicing with the hand as well as with other objects you can perceive the world from a completely new angle.

Look at your meditation instrument, then gaze through it in holo-mode. Go back and forth like this several times. This helps to flex the lens of the eye, and with practice you will be able to perfect the visuals. Feel the difference when the object appears solid and when it appears transparent.

While looking at your hand in holo-mode, close your eyes and visualize your whole body in that same transparent etheric state. Merge into that awareness. Feel yourself becoming transparent, translucent. Then try to extend that perception further into the environment surrounding you. With your eyes still closed, visualize the whole universe as a hologram of light.

To have a mini-session, all it takes is the raising of the hand(s) and going into a holo-mode for a few minutes. Full sessions should last 20 minutes or longer. I recommend doing this at least two to three times a week in combination with frequent daily mini-sessions.

The Holographic Exercises

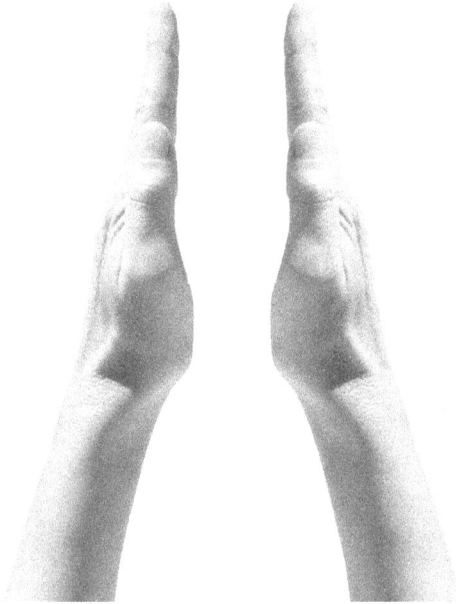

Step One

Turn your hands to face each other approximately 1/3 of an inch apart.

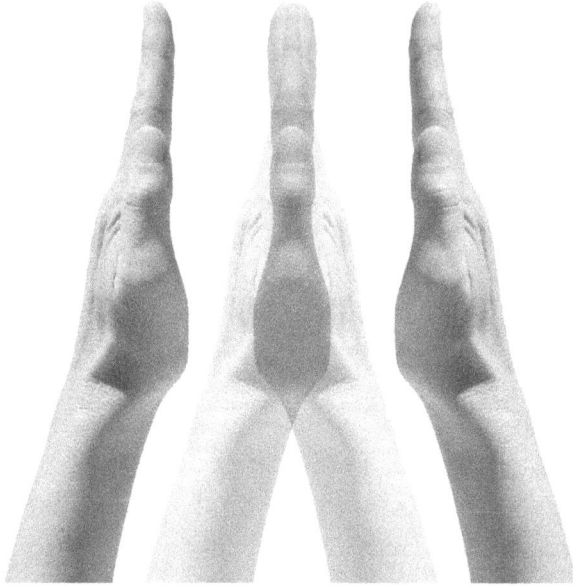

Step Two

Apply the Hologazing technique looking into the distance and witness the doubling effect and the hands' wave-like appearance. Observe the creation of a virtual shape in the middle, where the wave-like images of both hands overlap.

Commentary

Since the material world is holographic in nature, light waves overlap creating interference patterns as they leap into three-dimensionality, appearing solid. The visual imagery during Hologazing imitates this overlapping. This is a powerful path to understanding that the world exists as a hologram of light.

While Hologazing our hands change their normal solid appearance into double wave-like shapes. But if you then bring both hands together an inch or less apart so these shapes overlap, a third image appears in the middle. Even though this third shape is not solid, it nevertheless assumes some degree of "realness". For example, if you try looking through it you will realize it obscures objects in the background just as any solid object would.

This exercise is a home version of a holographic laboratory enabling us to observe with our own eyes the mysterious process of creating a virtual, holographic image out of thin air. Remember, we can experiment with any object as long as it's not wider than an inch or two. As I mentioned before, this has to do with the dynamics of vision. If the objects we are observing are too wide, the left and right visual fields will only partially overlap. With the practice of this meditation, we become more familiar with the holographic nature of our universe.

Human beings are highly visual creatures and this exercise is a visual mind-opener. It points to the idea that things are not always what they seem. This exercise gives us direct insight into how the eyes and the mind work together to create 3-D effects. When you hologaze, notice there are no words and no thoughts - just pure witnessing. It helps us grasp the truth of how we function in the world. To think holographically is to think holistically, to see the inherent wholeness of it all.

Practice Guidelines

Select a number of real-life objects (two of each) somewhere between 2-4 inches wide. For example - 2 coins, 2 thin candles, 2 leafs, 2 pens - and designate them as your meditation instruments. Take one object in each hand and bring them close together, about an inch apart. Then shift into holo-mode and observe the virtual hologram appearing in the middle, as a replica of the other two.

Hologaze at two different objects and see what happens when the visual fields overlap. Observe the various textures, colors and other characteristics of the interference pattern that is created between the two objects. Notice how the interference pattern looks solid and you cannot see the background. Work with a different pair of objects every day for a period of time.

Remember to do short and then longer meditations with your various objects. Visualize yourself and the world as a virtual hologram of light. Let this level of understanding sink into the deepest fabric of your awareness. Now Hologazing has begun to transform your worldview by bringing you closer to your true nature.

"The essence of the beautiful is unity in variety."

- W. Somerset Maugham

Applying Universal Values Of Oneness

Oneness Khi

Love Khi

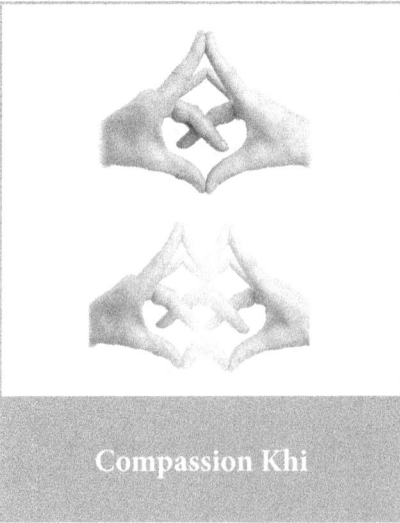

Compassion Khi

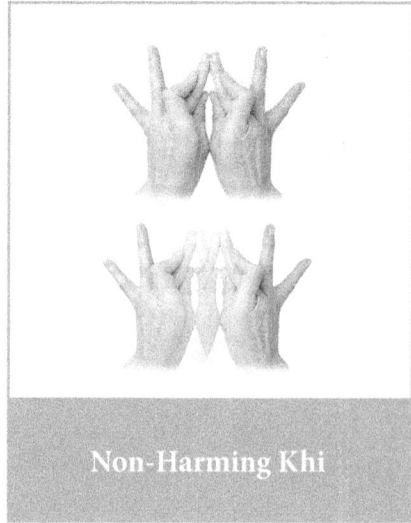

Non-Harming Khi

Four Holographic Meditation Khis

In this Chapter we are taking the art of Hologazing to a whole new experiential level. Instead of external objects, we will hologaze using geometric hand patterns in order to shift from the physical to the holographic form. In doing so, we create holographic Master Keys, also known as Khis.

In this part of the self-healing program, we are introducing four specific hand patterns. These Khis are used as meditation tools through which we can achieve Oneness, Love, Compassion and Non-Harming as a way of life. These concepts represent universal spiritual principles as well as major life themes. By living in accordance with them we can heal and improve our own life and consequently the lives of others.

The first step toward transformation is recognizing when our thoughts, emotions and actions are not in harmony with these principles. Then we can start correcting the imbalances through conscious efforts. The purpose of this four-step program of meditations is to first generate awareness by gaining deeper insight into their meaning; secondly, to consciously implement them through our actions and behavior; and finally, to heal any conflict in duality that inhibits embracing these spiritual qualities.

Oneness Khi

Love Khi

Compassion Khi

Non-Harming Khi

When we project Oneness, Love, Compassion and Non-Harming onto the outside world and see them reflected back to ourselves, we have achieved balance. If we are experiencing the opposite of those qualities, we need to look at the underlying cause. Antagonism, alienation, loneliness, anger and violence are signs of imbalance that ultimately originate within our own perception. The question is not just why someone is harming me or rejecting me, but why am I perceiving this. Of all the possibilities, why am I choosing this particular experience with my mind's eye?

Suffering can be caused by a lack of balanced perspective. A dualistic view and lack of clarity result in the loss of wholeness. Often, a simple shift in perception can release us from being stuck there. Meditation on the Khi is meditation on the middle road, the path of balance. To create the Khi, we join both our hands into an equal relationship. They represent the positive and negative polarities. Bringing the hands together is a move away from separation toward reunion. The transition into a holographic form merges the two opposites into a singularity which represents the act of reconciliation.

Healing at its root is an enlightening process. We dissolve our problems by seeing the truth, by becoming more conscious. The Khis help us attune our mind to the consciousness of Oneness, Love, Compassion and Non-Harming. Healing begins with meditation. Accessing inner wisdom we rid ourselves of views that hold us in self-limiting beliefs. We become what we think! By aligning our intention with Oneness, Love, Compassion and Non-Harming we become the embodiment of these divine attributes.

Because everything is interconnected, these kind of spiritual practices are not only good for us, but for the whole world. Holographically speaking, by changing our consciousness we are in fact impacting the whole. The positive changes in us will be simultaneously encoded in every cell, in every particle of everyone and everything in the universe. Even if we have achieved the mastery of these spiritual principles in ourselves, we can continuously contribute to the well-being of others by doing these practices. This is the ultimate act of universal compassion. By producing and spreading these thoughts and vibrations, we are shining a light, dissipating the darkness which envelopes us with ignorance and suffering. Knowing this gives us the means for transformation. And if more and more people willingly commit to changing themselves it could ignite a wave of transformation.

Practice Guidelines

Learning the Khis

Before we can practice meditation effectively, we first have to learn the Khi techniques outlined in this chapter. Instead of connecting the hands in an uneven fashion, our goal is to "snap" them together into perfect alignment. Any initial discomfort gradually falls away and the pattern fits like a glove. When creating the Khis, the fingers stretch, cross and connect at different touch points. The stimulation of pressure points increases the flow of chi and we feel a relaxing, healing effect. With each pose we discover a subtle mood, a soothing sensation caused by energies flowing harmoniously through the energetic seal. Though perhaps awkward at first, through repetition you'll find greater flexibility, coordination and finger dexterity. When you can strike a perfect pattern effortlessly, without thinking about it or with your eyes closed, you have learned the Khi.

The next step is learning the precise holographic forms displayed in the technique section. First we create the hand pose, bring it in front of our eyes, and then apply Hologazing. Unless the physical hand pattern is perfectly symmetrical, the holographic shape will appear uneven. To master the forms, it requires some patience and concentration. Hologazing at hand patterns is a sight-touch technique, simultaneously engaging our eyes and hands. Observing geometric shapes emerging is like watching a kaleidoscopic dance of balance. The multi-dimensional effects shift our perception and gently entice our mind into a meditative state. Once we have learned the techniques well, we can proceed with the practices.

Basic Exercise

The beginning exercise is a simple sequence consisting of slow movement coordinated with breathing.

Sit cross-legged with your hands on your knees. You can also sit on a chair or a sofa and rest your hands on your lap.

Select one meditation Khi and set your intention.

During a long slow inhalation, bring your hands apart.

While exhaling, slowly bring the hands together and fold them into the Khi. Then close your eyes while holding the pose. Breathe normally focusing on the hands for a short while.

Next, open the eyes and during a long slow inhalation, raise the hand pose in front of your eyes and begin Hologazing; continue for a brief while.

Then close your eyes and take in a deep breath. While exhaling, slowly bring the hands down and unclasp them, resting them on your your knees or on your lap.

Repeat this basic sequence a few more times, making the movements very slow and focused. Don't rush through it. Long, deep, slow inhalations and exhalations will release stress and tension, clearing your mind and relaxing you. Imagine the left and right side of your body are mirror reflections of each other. Align the poses to your middle, with the spine as a central axis. After just a few minutes you will feel more centered, grounded and connected. For best results, practice for 5-15 minutes. Upon completion of your exercise, close your eyes. Sit still or simply lie down, entering deeper meditation for a while longer.

A good time for practice is right before going to sleep, but make sure you are not too tired. Finish with your daily chores, so that you can relax and focus on your inner being. Upon completion of your meditation, don't engage in other activities before going to sleep. This will let you sleep deeply, which helps internalize the healing energies and the insights on a deeper subconscious level.

Another auspicious time is right upon awakening, when the mind is fresh and receptive. Align your intention with the Khi and try to maintain that focus throughout the day. Of course you can practice any other time that is convenient depending on your schedule. Practice each Khi for a few days, a week, or even a month, until you feel that you have achieved the desired results. Life is an unending process of transformation and you can continue to apply these tools throughout your life as you need them.

In this spiritual art the hands are the central feature, utilized as instruments for meditation. Think of your hands as divine lotuses through which chi, your life force, flows. By cleansing them before the practice, they become a purified instrument. Designate a special area or maybe create an altar in your home for your practice. The altar symbolizes a sacred place. Practicing at the same place builds up the energy and transforms it into a power vortex. External power places are also auspicious for practicing. They bring the sacred into the mundane, and can help deepen your meditation by providing a balanced environment. A power place can be a spiritual temple or a place of natural beauty such as a garden, a grassy hill, or the ocean.

Oneness Khi

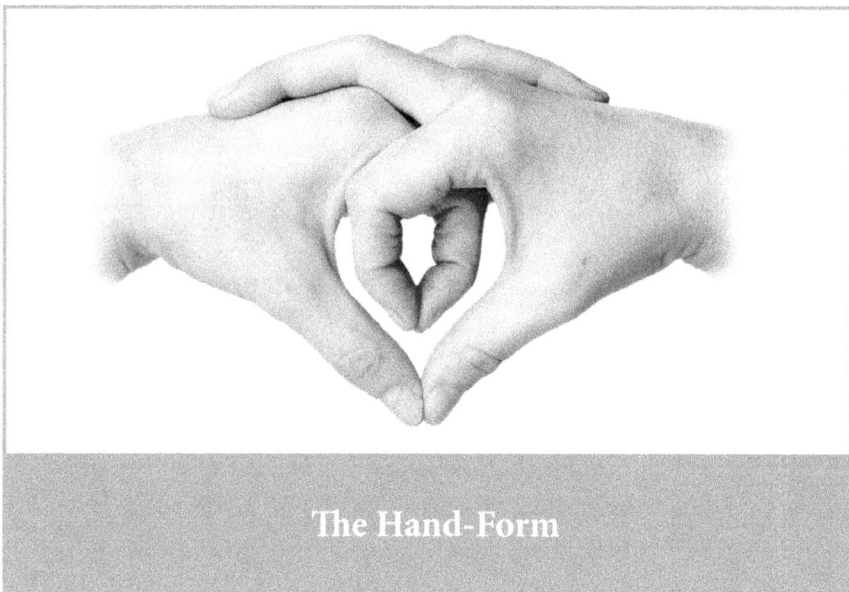

The Hand-Form

The Holo-Form

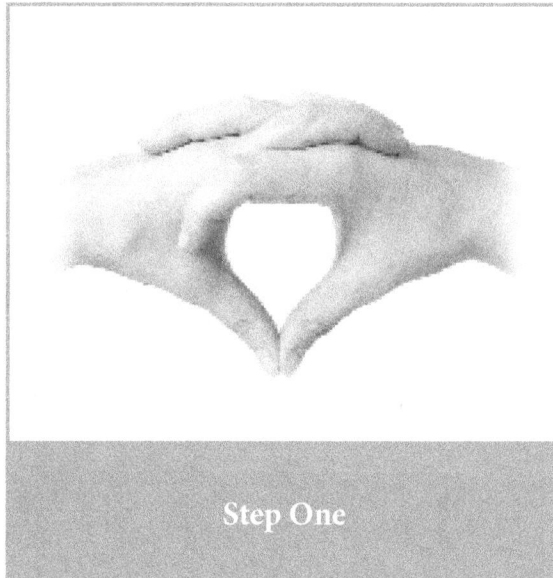

Step One

Interlace the fingers and connect the

thumbs, pointing downwards.

Step Two

Fold your index fingers

into a circle.

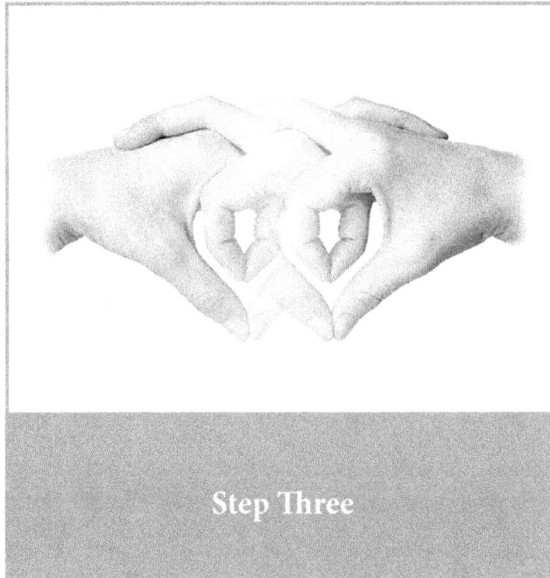

Step Three

Apply Hologazing.

Commentary

The hand-form of the Oneness Khi features a circle embraced by a larger circle, symbolizing that all created forms are part of the infinite source of spirit. When it shifts into the holographic form, the inner circle becomes double. Even though the emerging circles are seemingly separate identities, we see they are not fundamentally separate. They are eternally in a state of unity.

Oneness Meditation connects us to our source and our true self, healing feelings of loneliness and alienation. It also helps dissolve separatist attitudes and behavior and enhances our consciousness of unity.

Love Khi

The Hand-Form

The Holo-Form

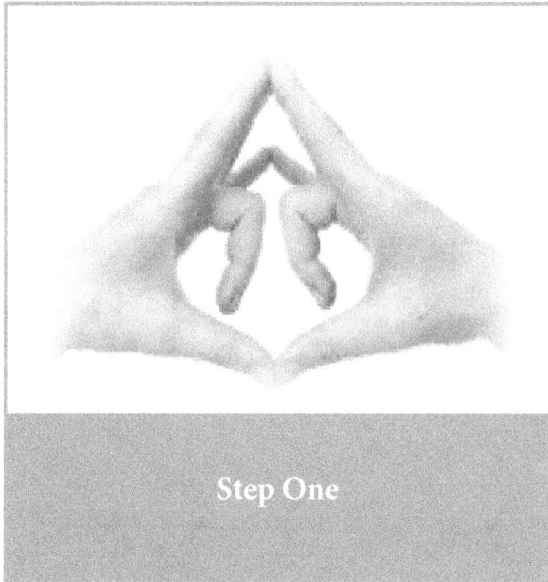

Step One

Connect all fingers at their tips, except
for the middle fingers.

Step Two

Place the middle fingers in the joint of
the thumbs.

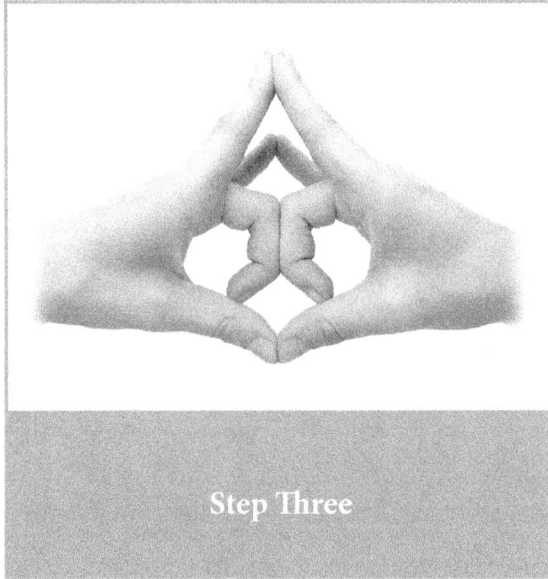

Step Three

Connect the middle fingers

back to back.

Step Four

Apply Hologazing.

Commentary

The hand-form of the Love Khi resembles a heart shape divided into its left and right heart chambers. When it shifts into the holographic form, a ring - an archetypal symbol of love - appears at the center. It is the ring which marries the polarities into a unified whole. It represents the liaison or the connecting link needed to bring individual halves together.

Love Meditation opens our spiritual heart, heals relationships and attracts love. It makes us kinder, more affectionate, and heals the emotional wounds of rejection and lack of self-worth.

Compassion Khi

The Hand-Form

The Holo-Form

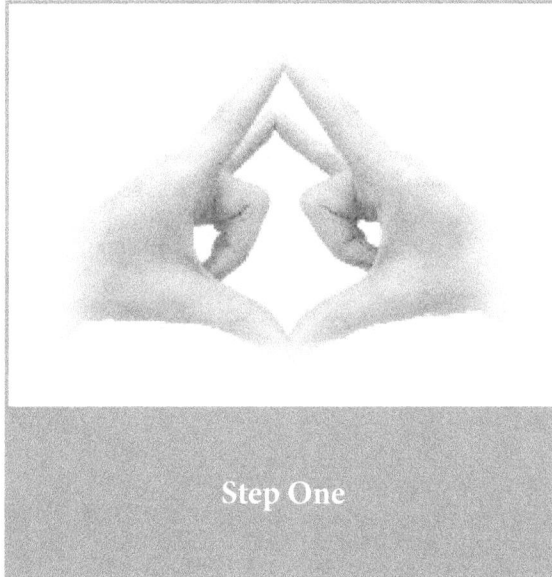

Step One

Connect the thumbs, index and pinky

fingers at their tips.

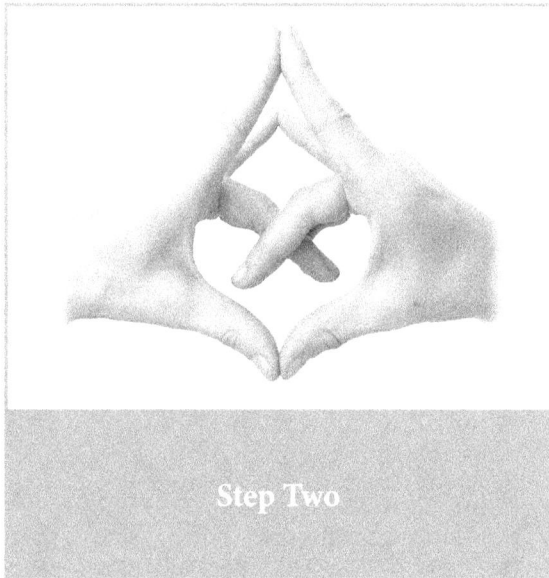

Step Two

Interlace the middle and ring fingers.

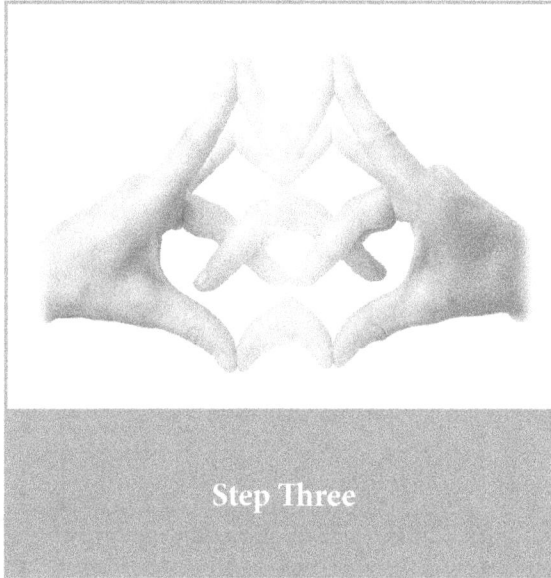

Step Three

Apply Hologazing.

Commentary

The hand-form of the Compassion Khi resembles a heart shape with an inscribed cross, carrying a message of help and mutual support. When it shifts into the holographic form, a circle emerges in the center of a criss-crossing pattern. This represents the common ground we all share. It alludes to the crossroads, a place where individual and collective interests come together in harmony. Out of compassion we temper personal goals in order to help each other.

Compassion Meditation awakens our spiritual heart, enhancing our sensitivity and empathy toward others. By increasing our social awareness and altruistic motivations, it frees us from suffering through the gift of compassion.

Non-Harming Khi

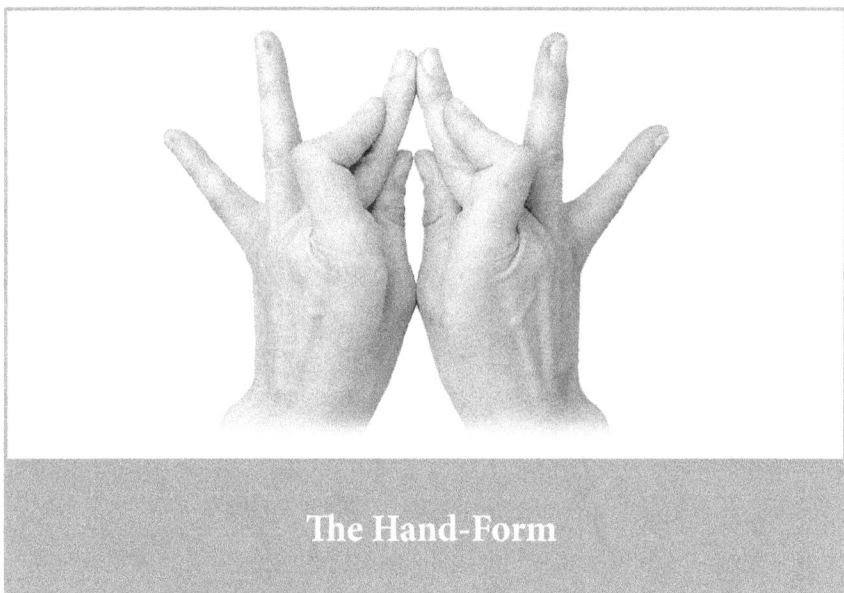

The Hand-Form

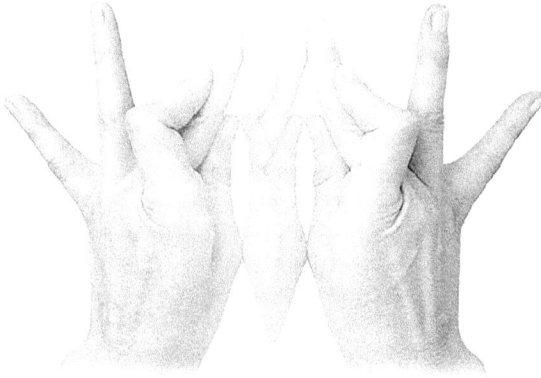

The Holo-Form

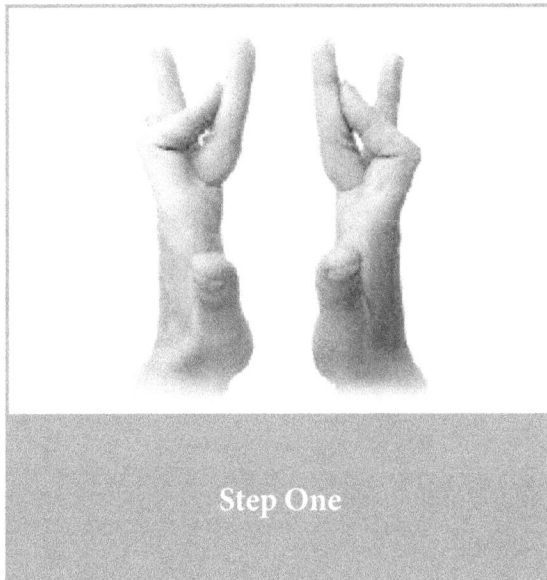

Step One

Place the index fingers on top of the
middle fingers and pull indexes slightly
backwards.

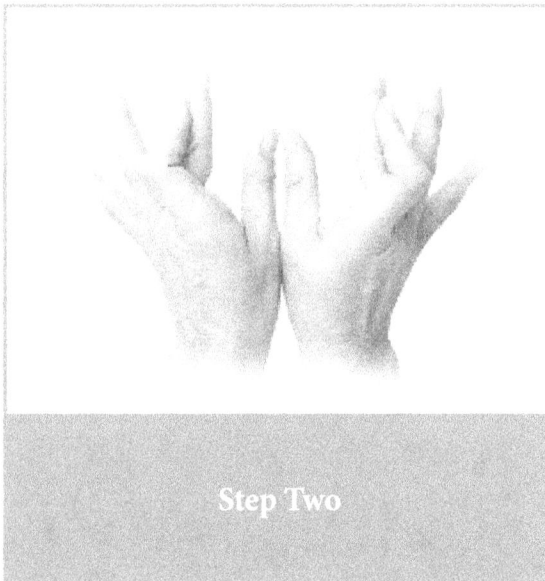

Step Two

Facing each other, connect the length of
both thumbs.

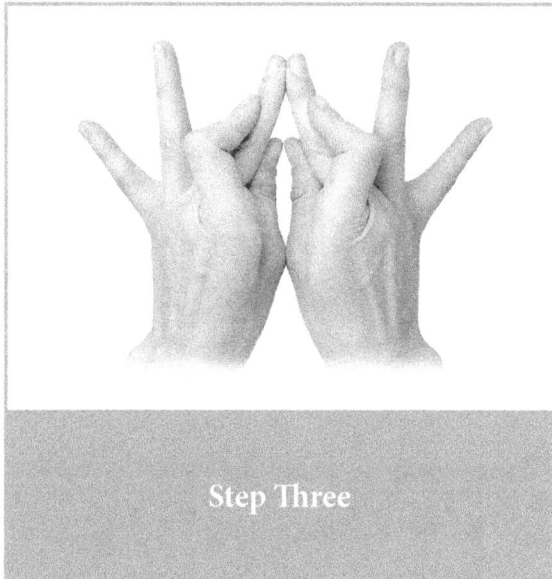

Step Three

Join the middle fingers, creating an
arrow in the middle. The ring and
pinky fingers will be pointing outwards.

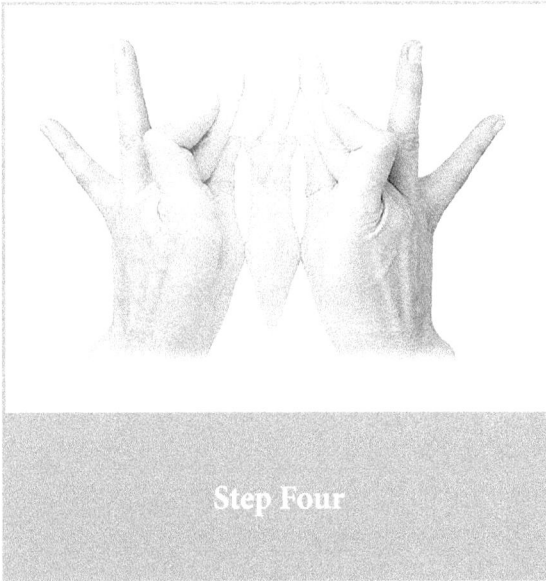

Step Four

Apply Hologazing.

Commentary

This hand-form of the Non-harming Khi resembles a sharp-edged shield of protection. In the center we see the outline of an arrow pointing outward, symbolizing an aggressive attitude and the destructive power that comes with it. When it becomes transformed into the holographic form, a reverse action can be observed: an inward-pointing arrow emerges and seems to cut into us like a knife. Just as the saying "what goes around, comes around" implies, the individual becomes the receiver of his or her own aggression.

Non-Harming Meditation develops composure and self-control. Protecting us from harm, it releases negative emotions such as rage and anger, then remolds and replaces aggressive behavior patterns with peace and equanimity.

Unity In Diversity

Despite all the suffering that exists, the Holographic Matrix is not evil by design. It's not as if there is a mean God up there tricking and trapping souls into a holographic web of illusions. Rather we are trapped by our own ignorance. Creation is truly a blessing, but it does come with strings attached. To rid ourselves of unhappiness and alienation we must live with right understanding.

The matrix is a cradle of infinite creative power from which everything is holographically projected into manifestation. It gives us life, though we often forget how special that is. Even though illusory on some level, it's beauty and power are breathtaking. If we allow it, we can be deluded into separation consciousness, but if we approach it as a magic holographic theatre full of opportunity, we can create positive experiences. It all depends on how we look at it, what we make out of it. If we understand the workings of the universe we can develop a more healthy worldview. We can give it a new meaning, and dream up a whole new reality.

Spirit is shear creative power of unfathomable magnitude. Universal intelligence is a force of progress, a constantly evolving design. Imagine the power, genius, wisdom and purposefulness that went into creating our holographic universe. It's here to please us, for our enjoyment and divine delight. We are sparks of that same intelligent force. To be creative, intelligent, purposeful and wise is to be awake and aware. We are human instruments using the resources available to create new worlds, civilizations, technologies and experiences right within the matrix.

Creativity is our birthright, our inherent nature. Our higher purpose is to make our world a better place. We are here to improve it, to care for it, and ultimately to be grateful for it. We are here to please, and to be pleased. And that joy and creativity springs forth effortlessly when we are in a state of harmony and accord, expressing love, peace, health and abundance in our lives. We are connected with our humanity and our true inner needs.

On a collective level, Oneness consciousness is the pursuit of universal goodness that frees us from the prison of pain and limitations. By doing things that benefit all, we automatically benefit. The question is not just what I can do for my personal aggrandizement, but what can I do to benefit the whole, because I am that spirit of Oneness. The happiness of others doesn't diminish our own, but adds value to our personal as well as our collective self-worth. So we should always delight in each others' well-being and achievements. Striving to open our eyes to Oneness lets us see clearly through the falsehood of envy, jealousy, malice and other self-defeating attitudes of separation.

The most brilliant example of Oneness consciousness is our own human body, with its trillions of cells working together unselfishly to sustain life. One for all - all for one. The human body is made up of tens of trillions of cells. While each cell is a separate unit with defined boundaries and space, they nevertheless gather together in several organ systems that share common traits and similarities. All these groups comprise a human body that functions as a whole. They work together, intelligently carrying out amazingly complex tasks and operations. For example, three billion messages are relayed to the brain every second, and our heart pumps about 7,000 liters of blood every day! This amazing system of intelligent communication and collaboration between the cells and organ systems keeps our multi-faceted selves in balance.

In the human body, there is an inherent sense of Oneness consciousness between the trillions of cell minds. There is no fundamental separation. The heart doesn't charge "for services rendered" or the liver for detoxifying the system. There is no manipulation for personal gain or control between individual cells or cell groups. If one cell begins to overpower others by replicating itself, it's called a cancer. It's unnatural. If one system weakens or goes down and remains untreated, all go down. Our body's natural harmony teaches us to embrace philanthropic principles of love and compassion.

If ten trillion cells can perform such complex functions and unselfishly work together in divine unison, why is it so hard for us all to find common ground and get along with each other? Through the Khi meditations we can learn to cooperate for the highest benefit of the world. After all, each one of us already embodies Unity consciousness. We don't need to look outside of us, it's encoded within us. All we have to do is listen to the innate wisdom of our own body-mind. When we meditate on the unifying intelligence that permeates every cell of our being, we awaken to the fact that we already are Oneness consciousness incarnate.

We all have the power to change, and our combined effort can create a mass shift toward a better life. Nothing can stop us but our ignorance, our lack of initiative to change and evolve. If we apply our creative imagination toward a more enlightened way of living, the result will inevitably be greater happiness and well-being.

Notes

1. -Gordon Fraser; Egil Lillestol; Inge Sellevag, Introduction by Stephen Hawking. *The Search for Infinity: Solving the Mysteries of the Universe* (New York: Facts On File, Inc., 1995), pp. 104-105.

2. -Fred Adams; Greg Laughlin, *The Five Ages of the Universe: Inside the Physics of Eternity* (New York: The Free Press, A Division of Simon & Schuster Inc., 1999), pp. 20-28.

3. -Christian De Duve, *Vital Dust: The Origin and Evolution of Life on Earth* (New York: Basic Books, A Subsidiary of Perseus Books, L.L.C.,1995), pp. 1-11.

4. -Ibid., pp. 46-82.

5. -David Bohm, *Wholeness and the Implicate Order* (London and New York: Routledge, 1995), p. 212.

6. -Jean Varenne, *Yoga and the Hindu Tradition* (Chicago and London: The University of Chicago Press, 1976), p. 18.

7. -Georg Feuerstein, Ph.D., *The Yoga Tradition: It's History, Literature, Philosophy and Practice* (Prescott, Arizona: Hohm Press, 1998), p. 225.

8. -Huston Smith, *The World's Religions: A Completely Revised and Updated Edition of The Religions of Man* (New York: Harper San Francisco, A Division of Harper Collins Publishers, 1991), pp. 196-220.

9. -Fritjof Capra, *The Tao of Physics* (Boston: Shambala, 1991), p.66.

10. Ibid., p. 73.

11. Ibid., pp. 69-70.

12. -Fred Unterseher; Jeannene Hansen; Bob Schlesinger, *Holography Handbook: Making Holograms the Easy Way* (Berkley, California: Ross Books, 1982), pp. 308-332.

13. -Steven Pinker, *How the Mind Works* (New York, London: W.W. Norton & Company, 1997), pp. 218-227.

14. -Michael Talbot, *The Holographic Universe* (New York: Harper Perennial, A Division of Harper Collins Publishers, 1992), p. 55.

15. -Ibid., p. 20.

16. -Gordon Fraser; Egil Lillestol; Inge Sellevag, Introduction by Stephen Hawking. *The Search for Infinity: Solving the Mysteries of the Universe* (New York: Facts On File, Inc., 1995), pp. 34-35

17. Ibid., pp. 36-37.

Bibliography

Adams, Fred; Laughlin, Greg. *The Five Ages of the Universe: Inside the Physics of Eternity.* New York: The Free Press, A Division of Simon & Schuster Inc., 1999.

Arguelles, Jose and Miriam. *Mandala.* Boston and London: Shambhala, 1995.

Bohm, David. *Wholeness and the Implicate Order.* London and New York: Routledge, 1995.

Bucke, Richard Maurice, M.D. *Cosmic Consciousness: A Study in the Evolution of the Human Mind.* New York: A Citadel Press Book, Published by Carol Publishing Group,1993.

Capra, Fritjof. *The Tao of Physics.* Third Edition, Updated. Boston: Shambala, 1991.

Cole, K.C. *First You Build a Cloud: And Other Reflections on Physics as a Way of Life.* San Diego, New York, London: Harcourt Brace & Company, 1999.

Davies, Paul. *God & The New Physics.* New York: A Touchstone Book, Published by Simon & Schuster, 1984.

Davies, Paul. *The 5th Miracle: The Search for the Origin and Meaning of Life.* New York, London, Sydney, Singapore: A Touchstone Book, Published by Simon & Schuster, 2000.

Duve, Christian De. *Vital Dust: The Origin and Evolution of Life on Earth.* New York: Basic Books, A Subsidiary of Perseus

Books, L.L.C.,1995.

Eliot, Charles. *Japanese Buddhism*. New York: Barnes & Noble, 1969.

Feuerstein, Georg, Ph.D. Foreword by Ken Wilber. *The Yoga Tradition: It's History, Literature, Philosophy and Practice*. Prescott, Arizona: Hohm Press, 1998.

Feuerstein, Georg, Ph.D.; *The Path of Ecstasy*. Boston & London: Shambhala, 1997.

Feuerstein, Georg, Ph.D.; and Miller, Jeanine. *The Essence of Yoga: Essays on the Development of Yogic Philosophy from the Vedas to Modern Times*. Rochester, Vermont: Inner Traditions International, 1998.

Fontana, Dr. David. *The Meditator's Handbook: A Comprehensive Guide to Eastern & Western Meditation Techniques*. Boston, MA: Element, 1998.

Fraser, Gordon; Lillestol, Egil; Sellevag, Inge. Introduction by Stephen Hawking. *The Search for Infinity: Solving the Mysteries of the Universe*. New York: Facts On File, Inc., 1995.

Govinda, Lama Anagarika. *Foundations of Tibetan Mysticism*. York Beach, Maine: Samuel Wiser, Inc., 1969.

Greene, Brian. *The Elegant Universe: Superstrings, Hidden Dimensions, and the Quest for the Ultimate Theory*. New York:

Vintage Books, A Division of Random House, Inc., 2000.

Grof, Stanislav, M.D.; Bennett, Hal Zina, Ph.D. *The Holotropic Mind: The Three Levels of Human Consciousness and How They Shape Our Lives.* Harper San Francisco, A Division of Harper Collins Publishers, 1993.

Hawking, Stephen. *A Brief History of Time. The Updated and Expanded Tenth Anniversary Edition.* New York: Bantam Books, 1998.

H.H. The Dalai Lama. *Ethics For The New Millennium.* New York: Riverhead Books, A Member of Penguin Putnam Inc., 1999.

H.H. The Dalai Lama. *A Simple Path. Basic Buddhist Teachings by His Holiness The Dalai Lama.* London: Thorsons, An Imprint of Harper Collins Publishers, 2000.

H.H. The Dalai Lama; Tsong-ka-pa & Hopkins, Jeffrey. *Deity Yoga: In Action and Performance Tantra.* Ithaca, New York: Snow Lion Publications, 1987.

Holden, Alan. *The Nature of Solids.* New York: Dover Publications, Inc., 1992.

Jung, Carl G. *Man and his Symbols.* New York: Anchor Books, Doubleday, 1964.

Khanna, Madhu. Yantra: *The Tantric Symbol of Cosmic Unity.*

New York: Thames and Hudson Inc., 1997.

Lawlor, Robert. *Sacred Geometry: Philosophy and Practice.* New York: Thames and Hudson Inc., 1998.

Levenson, Claude B. *Symbols of Tibetan Buddhism.* Paris, France: Editions Assouline, 1996.

Maharishi Mahesh Yogi. *Science of Being and Art of Living: Transcendental Meditation.* New York: Meridian, 1963.

Maharishi Mahesh Yogi. *Transcendental Meditation.* New York: Donald I. Fine, Inc., 1994.

McDonald, Kathleen. *How To Meditate: A Practical Guide.* Somerville, Massachusetts: Wisdom Publications, 1984.

Monaghan, Patricia, and Viereck, Eleanor G. *Meditation: The Complete Guide.* Novato, California: New World Library, 1999.

Neumann, Erich. *The Origins and History of Consciousness.* Princeton, N.J.: Princeton University Press, 1995.

Park, David. *The Fire Within The Eye: A Historical Essay On The Nature And Meaning of Light.* Princeton, New Jersey: Princeton University Press, 1999.

Pinker, Steven. *How the Mind Works.* New York, London: W.W. Norton & Company, 1997.

Pribram, Karl. *Languages of the Brain.* Monterey, California: Wadsworth Publishing, 1997.

Reed, Henry, Ph.D. *Awakening Your Psychic Powers.* New York: St. Martin's Paperbacks, 1996.

Ronchi, Vasco. *Optics: The Science of Vision.* New York: Dover Publications, Inc., 1991.

Saunders, E. Dale. *Mudra: A Study of Symbolic Gestures in Japanese Buddhist Sculpture.* Princeton, New Jersey: Bollingen Series LVIII, Princeton University Press, 1985.

Schiffer, Fredric, M.D. *Of Two Minds: The Revolutionary Science of Dual-Brain Psychology.* New York: The Free Press, A Division of Simon &Schuster Inc., 1998.

Schimmel, Annemarie. *The Mystery of Numbers.* New York, Oxford: Oxford University Press, 1993.

Smith, Huston. *The World's Religions: A Completely Revised and Updated Edition of The Religions of Man.* New York: Harper San Francisco, A Division of Harper Collins Publishers, 1991.

Talbot, Michael. *The Holographic Universe.* New York: Harper Perennial, A Division of Harper Collins Publishers, 1992.

Talbot, Michael. *Mysticism and the New Physics.* London: Arkana, Penguin Books, 1993.

Tattersall, Ian. *Becoming Human: Evolution & Human Uniqueness*. New York, San Diego, London: Harcourt Brace & Company, 1998.

Unterseher, Fred; Hansen, Jeannene; Schlesinger, Bob. *Holography Handbook: Making Holograms the Easy Way*. Berkley, California: Ross Books, 1982.

Varenne, Jean. *Yoga And the Hindu Tradition*. Chicago and London: The University of Chicago Press, 1976.

Walker, Evan Harris. *The Physics of Consciousness: The Quantum Mind and the Meaning of Life*. Cambridge, Massachusetts: Perseus Books, 1999.

Wolf, Fred Alan. *Taking the Quantum Leap: The New Physics For Non-Scientists*. New York: Harper & Row, 1989.

Wolf, Fred Alan, Ph.D. *The Spiritual Universe: One Physicist's Vision of Spirit, Soul, Matter, and Self*. Portsmouth, NH: Moment Point Press, Inc., 1999.

Wolf, Fred Alan, Ph.D.; *The Dreaming Universe: A Mind-Expanding Journey Into The Realm Where Psyche & Physics Meet*. New York: A Touchstone Book, Published by Simon & Schuster, 1994.

Wyller, Dr. Arne A. *The Creating Consciousness: Science as the Language of God*. Denver, Colorado: Divina, A Division of MacMurray & Beck, 1999.

Zohar, Danah. *The Quantum Self: Human Nature and Consciousness Defined By The New Physics.* New York: Quill/William Morrow, 1990.

Zohar, Fanah; Marshall, Ian. *The Quantum Society: Mind, Physics, and a New Social Vision.* New York: Quill, William Morrow, 1994.

Zukav, Gary. *The Dancing Wu Li Masters: An Overview of the New Physics.* New York: Bantam Books, 1980.

www.ingramcontent.com/pod-product-compliance
Lightning Source LLC
LaVergne TN
LVHW051647080426
835511LV00016B/2532